WASHINGTON IRVING'S
SUNNYSIDE

SLEEPY HOLLOW RESTORATIONS

Tarrytown • New York

1. *Washington Irving,* oil on canvas by John Wesley Jarvis
(1769–1830), New York City, 1809.
Irving was 26 at the time.

WASHINGTON IRVING'S

SUNNYSIDE

by Joseph T. Butler

The Irving family seal carries the Latin motto
Sub sole sub umbra Virens ("flourishing in the sun and in the
shade"). This photograph is taken from one of Irving's watch fobs.

Sleepy Hollow Restorations, Incorporated, is a nonprofit educational institution chartered by the State of New York. It was established under an endowment provided by the late John D. Rockefeller, Jr. Sleepy Hollow Restorations owns and maintains Van Cortlandt Manor, in Croton-on-Hudson, a distinguished eighteenth-century family residence; Sunnyside, Washington Irving's picturesque home in Tarrytown; and Philipsburg Manor, Upper Mills, an impressive example of a colonial commercial-mill complex in North Tarrytown.

ISBN 0-912882-13-1, cloth
ISBN 0-912882-12-3, paper
Library of Congress Catalog Card Number: 74-6757

Printed in the United States of America
Designed by Ray Freiman

Sunnyside from the Hudson, oil on canvas, artist unknown,
c. 1850. This work shows the familiar sight of Irving's home,
the river edge tracks of the Hudson River Railroad and,
at the left, the steamboat, "Washington Irving" the
Hudson River Day Line's large, steel passenger ship.

Continuing Irving's tradition of welcoming guests from this country and abroad, guides greet visitors touring the house and grounds of Sunnyside, restored to its mid-nineteenth-century appearance.

WASHINGTON IRVING will always occupy an important place in the history of American literature. Although he owed much to European literary sources for his inspiration, he was certainly the most polished and one of the best known American writers of his day. It was through his shorter works, such as "The Legend of Sleepy Hollow" and "Rip Van Winkle," which are as fresh and charming today as when they were written, that Irving provided the first mature examples of American fiction. While some of his books, by today's standards, seem relatively difficult to read, his reputation is well established through his lighter and more eloquent short stories and sketches.

Born in New York City on April 3, 1783, Washington Irving was the eleventh and last child of Scottish-English parents. When Irving was young, his father had a highly successful mercantile business. The boy's early life was sheltered because he was sickly. His great enjoyments were the theater, music, art, travel, and social occasions; he spent much time sitting on the New York docks watching ships passing. Irving's brother Peter owned a newspaper, the *Morning Chronicle;* and when Irving was nineteen, and studying law, he contributed a series of essays dealing largely with the theater. Characteristic of his later work, he signed a pseudonym in the eighteenth-century manner, "Jonathan Oldstyle."

Irving traveled in Europe between 1804 and 1806 and curiously paid little attention to the Napoleonic wars or indeed to politics in general. Traveling was good for both his health and his spirit. He met such notables as the French writer Madame de Staël, and the American artist Washington Allston; and in London he saw Mrs. Sarah Siddons, the tragic actress, at Covent Garden.

Upon his return to New York, Irving continued reading law and was eventually admitted to the bar. Shortly thereafter he began work on a series of humorous stories about contemporary New York life for the *Salmagundi,* a periodical which ran for twenty numbers in 1807 and 1808. He was joined in this venture by his brothers Peter and William, and James Kirke Paulding, William's brother-in-law. Since none of these essays is individually signed, it is impossible to ascribe any with certainty to Washington Irving. Encouraged by his brother, Irving worked on a more extended project which was called *A History of New York, from the Beginning of the World to the End of the Dutch Dynasty. Containing, Among Many Surprising and Curious Matters the Unutterable Ponderings of Walter the Doubter; The Disastrous Projects of William the Testy; and the Chivalric Achievements of Peter the Headstrong; The Three Dutch Governors of New Amsterdam; being the only Authentic History of the Times that hath ever been published. By Diedrich Knickerbocker;* it was eventually published in 1809. The *Knickerbocker History* is a satire on the old Dutch families of New Netherland. It is such an elaborate and intricate composition, filled with historical anecdotes, that it must have taken Irving away from the law for great spans of time.
(Plates frontispiece [1], 2, 3)

During this period, Irving was very much involved in the congenial young literary and artistic set of New York. Always at ease with large groups of people, he greatly enjoyed social functions. One of the tragedies in Irving's life was his strong attachment to Matilda Hoffman, the daughter of Josiah Ogden Hoffman, in whose office he had studied law. Irving was apparently deeply fond of her and remained a bachelor after her early death in 1809. He wrote: "Her image was continually before me, and I dreamt of her incessantly."[1]

2. *Confrontation of Risingh and Von Poffenburgh at Fort Casimer,* Illustration for Irving's *A History of New York . . . by Diedrich Knickerbocker,* wash drawing by George Cruikshank (1792–1878), London, c. 1835.

3. *Diedrich Knickerbocker* (frontispiece illustration, Irving's *A History of New York . . . by Diedrich Knickerbocker*), wash drawing, by Felix O. C. Darley (1822–1888), New York City, c. 1848–1854.

In 1815 Irving and his brother Peter were sent by their family to Liverpool, where they found their business to be in great disorder. It was during this stay, actually in 1817, that Irving visited Sir Walter Scott at his estate, Abbotsford, in Scotland. By 1818 the Irving mercantile firm was bankrupt. William Irving, now in Congress, tried to secure government appointments for his brothers stranded in England. One was forthcoming for Washington, but he declined it on the basis that his talents were purely literary. This forced upon Washington Irving the decision to become a full-time author. At this time Irving was probably so much motivated toward writing that a minor governmental post did not appeal. Later, with maturity and success in his writing, Irving did accept several prestigious government appointments.

He immediately set to work and the results of his efforts were quite impressive: *The Sketch Book,* published serially in 1819 and 1820; *Bracebridge Hall,* in Germany and France between 1822 and 1825; and after a stay in Spain as an attaché at the United States Legation in Madrid, *The Life and Voyages of Christopher Columbus,* in 1828 in three volumes; in 1829 he published *A Chronicle of the Conquest of Granada.* (Plates 4 through 13)

4. *The Author of the Sketch Book,* engraving by
   William Keenan (c. 1810–1855), published by
   E. Littell, Philadelphia, c. 1820. Irving was 37 when
   this was done. The seal and sealing wax box
   which Irving is holding are shown on page 10.

5. *Washington Irving*, oil on canvas by Gilbert Stuart
Newton (1794–1835), London, England, spring, 1820.

6. *Rip's Vision* by Augustus Hoppin, wood engraving
   by Richardson & Cox, from *The Sketch Book,*
   G. P. Putnam & Sons, New York, 1864.

7. From *Rip Van Winkle,* The American Art-Union,
   designed and etched by Felix O. C. Darley (1822–1888), 1848.

Rip Van Winkle.

a posthumous writing of Diedrich Knickerbocker

By Woden, God of Saxons,
From whence comes Wensday. that is Wodensday,
Truth is a thing that ever I will keep
Unto thylke day in which I creep into
My sepulchre —
                              Cartwright.

Whoever has made a voyage up the
Hudson must remember the Kat-
Kaalskill mountains. They are a dis-
membered branch of the great appalla-
chian family, and are seen away to the
west of the river swelling up to a noble
height and lording it over the surroun-
ding country. Every change of season
every change of weather, indeed every hour
of the day, produces some change in the
magical hues and shapes of these mountains, and they are regarded by all the

8. Manuscript page from "Rip Van Winkle,"
from The Washington Irving Collection,
C. W. Barrett Library, University of Virginia Library.

9. From *The Legend of Sleepy Hollow*, designed and
   etched by Felix O. C. Darley (1822–1888),
   American Art-Union, New York, 1848.

10. *Ichabod Crane at a Ball at Van Tassel's Mansion*
    (illustration from "The Legend of Sleepy Hollow"), oil on
    canvas, by John Quidor (1801–1881), New York City, 1855.

The legend of Sleepy Hollow.

/ Found among the papers of the late Diedrich
Knickerbocker /

A pleasing land of drowsy head it was,
Of dreams that wave before the half shut eye;
And of gay castles in the clouds that pass,
Forever flushing round a summer sky.

Castle of Indolence?

In the bosom of one of the spa-
cious coves which indent the eastern
shore of the Hudson, at that broad
expansion of the river denominated
by the ancient Dutch navigators of
those waters the Tappaan Zee, and
            prudently
where they always shortened sail
and implored the protection of St. Nicholas
when they crossed, there lies a small
market town or rural port, which
by some is called Greensburgh, but
which is more universally and
properly known by the name of

---

11. First page of the only known manuscript of
    The Legend of Sleepy Hollow.
    The New York Public Library, Berg Collection.

12. *Ichabod Crane and the Headless Horseman*
(illustration of "The Legend of Sleepy Hollow," from
Washington Irving's *The Sketch Book of Geoffrey
Crayon, Gent.*), color lithograph by C. E. Lewis
after painting by William John Wilgus
(1819–1853), published by A. W. Wilgus in Buffalo, c. 1857.

13. *Washington Irving,* pencil drawing bearing the monogram of Sir Thomas Lawrence (1769–1830), England, c. 1828–1830.

From 1829 until 1832 he acted as Secretary of the United States Legation in London. He continued to write, and the results were the publication of the *Voyages and Discoveries of the Companions of Columbus* (1831) and the *Alhambra,* known as the "Spanish Sketch Book" (1832). (Plates 14, 15)

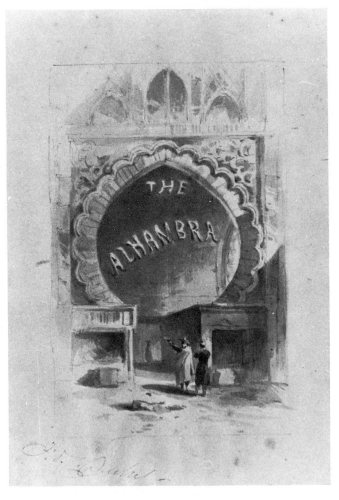

14. *Frontispiece, The Alhambra,* wash drawing by Felix O. C. Darley (1822–1888), New York City, c. 1848.

15. *Illustration for "Aben Habuz, the Arabian
Astrologer, and the Christian Princess,"* for
Washington Irving's *The Alhambra,* wash drawing,
by Felix O. C. Darley (1822–1888),
New York City, c. 1848.

Irving, through social connections and literary friends, could feel at home in London, Paris, Dresden, or Madrid. He met most of the important social, artistic, and literary people and did well financially at this time. He was an enormous success because he brought to America a new feeling of respect, the respect of authorship which was greatly admired. Although Irving worked very hard, he wished to preserve the idea that writing was a gentlemanly pursuit that could be accomplished with the left hand.

In 1832 Irving returned to the United States after an absence of seventeen years. He traveled in the midwest and especially through Missouri. On September 13, 1832, he wrote to his sister Mrs. Catherine Paris from St. Louis:

My Dear Sister:

I wrote to you from Cincinnati, which place I left in a steamboat on the 3d inst., and arrived the next day at Louisville, Ky. There we embarked in another steamboat, and continued down the Ohio to its confluence with the Mississippi, when we ascended the latter river to this place, where we arrived late last night. Our voyage was prolonged by our repeatedly running aground in the Ohio from the lowness of the water. Twice we remained aground for the greater part of twenty-four hours. The last evening of our voyage we were nearly run down and sent to the bottom by a huge steamboat, the "Yellow Stone," which came surging down the river under the impetus of "high pressure" and a rapid current. Fortunately our pilot managed the helm so as to receive the blow obliquely, which tore away part of a wheel, and staved in all the upper works of one side of our boat. We made shift to limp through the remainder of our voyage, which was but about twelve miles. I have been charmed with the grand scenery of these two mighty rivers. We have had splendid weather to see them in—golden sunshiny days, and serene moonlight nights. The magnificence of the Western forests is quite beyond my anticipations; such gigantic trees, rising like stupendous columns—and then the abundance of flowers and flowering shrubs. . . .[2]

In 1835, the same year that he purchased his country house, Sunnyside, he published *The Crayon Miscellany* in three parts. It included *A Tour on the Prairies, Abbotsford and Newstead Abbey,* a travel book with fine anecdotes of these houses, and *Legends of the Conquest of Spain.*

Irving's interest in America emerged again in 1836 with the publication of *Astoria,* which was written with the assistance of his nephew, Pierre; he was fascinated by John Jacob Astor and the development of his great fur empire. This success was followed in 1837 with the appearance of *Adventures of Captain Bonneville.* The following year, because of his great public success and popularity, the Democratic Party considered him as a candidate for Mayor of New York and President Van Buren offered him the cabinet post of Secretary of the Navy; Irving declined both of these honors.

Between 1839 and 1841 the writer spent a highly productive time and contributed 30 essays and stories to the *Knickerbocker Magazine.* In 1841 he published an unusual work, *Biography and Physical Remains of the Late Margaret Miller Davidson.* It dealt with the life of a New York State child poet, who lived between 1822 and 1838. Margaret Miller was only two and one-half years younger than Matilda Hoffman when she died. In 1842, Irving was appointed Envoy Extraordinary and Minister Plenipotentiary to the Court of Spain by President Tyler. This post he did accept and remained in it until 1846. That year he returned to the United States to his house, Sunnyside, at Tarrytown, where he began to

16. *Washington Irving and His Little Dog*, pencil sketch
by Felix O. C. Darley (1822–1888), New York City, July, 1848.

work on his monumental biography, *Life of George Washington*. (Plate 16) Other works also began to flow from his pen. In 1849, *Oliver Goldsmith: A Biography* appeared; and in that year and the following, a two-volume work dealing with Spanish history, *Mahomet and His Successors*, was written. In 1855, *Wolfert's Roost* was published, and in the same year Volumes 1 and 2 of the *Life of George Washington*. (Plates 17, 18, 19, 20, 21) This great work was finished and Volume 5 had just been published when Irving died at Sunnyside on November 28, 1859. His funeral was held at Christ Episcopal

Church in Tarrytown, New York, and he was buried in Sleepy Hollow Cemetery, Tarrytown. A contemporary description of his funeral noted: "Thousands from far and near silently looked for the last time on his genial face, and mourned his loss as that of a personal friend and national benefactor."[3]

17. *Miniature-portrait of Washington Irving* by William J. Henry Powell (1823–1879), oil on ivory, Sunnyside, 1855. Irving was 72 when this was painted.

18. *The Chieftain and the Child,* watercolor by George B. Butler, 1854. The child, Washington Irving, is shown meeting George Washington.

19. *The Young Washington,* wash drawing by
Felix O. C. Darley (1822–1888). Engraving appears in
Life of Washington, Volume 1, chapter 4, 1856.

20. Photograph of *Washington Irving at Sunnyside,*
from F. Langenheim stereoscopic slide, 1856.
Irving was 73 when the photograph was taken.

As a literary figure Irving is certainly most significant because he brought American fiction into the mainstream of world literature. Completely involved with the Romantic movement, Irving owed much to Sir Walter Scott, whom he greatly admired and, as mentioned, with whom he had spent several days at the former's neo-Gothic house, Abbotsford, as well as seeing him in London in 1830. In addition, he was also influenced by Fielding, Sterne, Goldsmith, Addison, and Steele. He was intimately aware of the work of his immediate predecessors and wrote with the complete knowledge that he was sometimes highly imitative of their style. The German Romantics, such as Ludwig Tieck and E. T. A. Hoffman, were also quite important in influencing the writings of Irving, who had a great fondness for German literature and for Italian and German music, opera in particular. While much of his work is certainly derivative, it is Irving's extraordinary feeling for folklore and his descriptions of landscape and local customs and the eccentricities of human beings as they are looking at the world that make him important. He constantly refused to take either himself or the society in which he lived completely seriously. He represents an extremely delicate balance between conformity and independence which, if not original in the strictest sense, is still creative and highly individual.

It is through the development of Irving's country property, Sunnyside, that the maturity of his interest in European Romanticism can be traced. In 1835 Washington Irving purchased a small property, eventually to encompass 24 acres, along the banks of the Hudson River, about 25 miles north of Manhattan, near present-day Tarrytown.

Tarrytown in 1835 was a quiet, sleepy country town. A local resident described it as small, dull, and unprogressive. There were only several retail stores which sold

21. *Washington Irving*, photograph by
Mathew B. Brady (1823–1896), New York City, c. 1859.
Probably taken shortly before Irving's death.
Collection of New-York Historical Society.

groceries, cloth, chinaware, liquor and tools; one small lumberyard; one or two shoemakers; and a blacksmith. The residents met one another in the street, in the stores, or in church. Otherwise, there was little entertainment. The main point of congregation and the only center of what might be termed any social activity was the store of Tommy Dean at Main Street and Broadway, where the local farmers congregated to transact business and to gossip. Dean's store also housed the post office; so at one time or another it was necessary for virtually everyone to come there.

Many changes had taken place by 1840. In that year Irving wrote to his sister Sarah:

You would hardly recognize Tarrytown, it has undergone such changes. These have in a great degree taken place since I have pitched my tent in the neighborhood. My residence here has attracted others; cottages and country seats have sprung up along the banks of the Tappan Sea, and Tarrytown has become the metropolis of quite a fashionable vicinity. When you knew the village, it was little better than a mere hamlet, crouched down at the foot of a hill, with its dock for the accommodation of the weekly market sloop. Now it has mounted the hill; boasts of its hotels, and churches of various denominations; has its little Episcopalian church with an organ, the gates of which, on Sundays, are thronged with equipages belonging to families resident within ten or a dozen miles along the river banks. We have, in fact, one of the most agreeable neighborhoods I ever resided in. Some of our neighbors are here only for the summer, having their winter establishments in town; others remain in the country all the year. We have frequent gatherings at each other's houses, without parade or expense, and I do not know when I have seen more delightful little parties, or more elegant little groups of females. We have, occasionally, excellent music, for several of the neighborhood have been well taught, have good voices, and acquit themselves well both with harp and piano; and our parties always end with a dance. We have picnic parties also, sometimes in some inland valley or piece of wood, sometimes on the banks of the Hudson, where some repair by land, and others by water. You would be delighted with these picturesque assemblages, on some wild woodland point jutting into the Tappan Sea, with gay groups on the grass under the trees; carriages glistening through the woods; a yacht with flapping sails and fluttering streamers anchored about half mile from shore, and rowboats plying to and from it, filled with lady passengers. . . .[4]

22. *The Old Cottage Taken Previous to Improvement,* watercolor attributed to George Harvey (c. 1800/01–1878), c. 1835. The cottage which Irving bought was actually a tenant house on Philipsburg Manor in the late seventeenth century. It was typical of country architecture of that time.

In 1798, because of a yellow fever epidemic in New York City, Irving had visited near Tarrytown at Paulding Manor, which was situated near Requa Landing. His friends, the Paulding family, owned large acreage and Irving saw the cottage, destined to be known as Sunnyside, standing on a promontory overlooking the Hudson during this visit. The old house had been built in the late seventeenth century in the typical country farmhouse architecture of the time. (Plate 22) Actually, the original house had been constructed for tenants on Philipsburg Manor, Upper Mills, the manor house of which is in present-day North Tarrytown. During the eighteenth century it had been owned by a branch of the Van Tassel family which Irving had immortalized in his "Legend of Sleepy Hollow" through characters which included Katrina Van Tassel. Irving had visited the Sleepy Hollow area as a child and was always deeply impressed by its romantic atmosphere with deep forests, mountains coming down to the banks of the river, and the colonial New York architecture still to be found there.

Between 1835 and 1837 Irving began to create a romantic dwelling from the old farmhouse. It was situated high on a steep bank looking down the Hudson River toward Manhattan and in front of it was an inlet where boats could be tied. The architecture of the house was conceived in a highly personal style. It must be remembered that Irving was remodeling his home at a period when much romantic and revival architecture was being conceived and constructed in England. Sunnyside has often been described as a Victorian house; yet, this is in no way an accurate reference. Irving built Dutch stepped gables at either end of the house and surmounted them with ancient weathervanes which came from old buildings in New York City and Albany. He also used several of the popular revival styles of the day, such as Gothic

23. *Sunnyside, the Van Tassel House, Residence of Washington Irving* from John W. Barker and Henry Howe, *Historic Collections of the State of New York,* 1842. This illustration and number 24 show Sunnyside after its first period of remodeling by Irving and Harvey. The stepped gables and entryway have been added.

24. *The Van Tassel house, the residence of Washington Irving, Esq.* watercolor by George Harvey (c. 1800/01–1878), c. 1836–1840.

and Romanesque, in providing architectural features for other parts of the house. (Plates 23, 24, 25)

Irving's good friend, the painter George Harvey, (c. 1800/01–1878) who lived nearby in Hastings-on-Hudson, greatly aided in the remodeling of the house and furnished many of its details. It is interesting to note that there was no architect for the remodeling project. Rather, Irving's ideas were transmitted to Harvey, who dealt with workmen at the site, as did Irving himself.

25. *Scudding Clouds after a Shower,* watercolor of Sunnyside, by George Harvey (c. 1800/01–1878), c. 1836–1840. This view of the riverside of Sunnyside shows the striped awnings which were used on the house during the summer.

Irving wrote to his brother Pierre in 1836:

I am living most cozily and delightfully in this dear, bright little home, which I have fitted up to my own humor. Everything goes on cheerily in my little household, and I would not exchange the cottage for any chateau in Christendom. I am working, too, with almost as much industry and rapidity as I did at Hell Gate, and, I think, will more than pay for my nest, from the greater number of eggs I shall be able to hatch there.[5]

26. *Washington Irving's House on the Hudson,* crayon drawing by Felix O. C. Darley (1822–1888). Dated July 24, 1848, it shows the house with the tower addition completed in 1847.

Ten years later (1847), because the house could no longer accommodate the large number of guests who visited Irving and his family who lived with him, a three-story tower with a slanting roof was added, which was referred to by many of his friends and contemporary sources as the "Pagoda." (Plates 26, 27, 28, 29) The area had four rooms which were occupied by servants and sometimes by overflow guests. About this time a bathroom and picture gallery were added to the rear of the house on the first floor, as well as some service rooms in the kitchen area, and a coal cellar.

27. *Sunnyside,* oil on canvas, by George Inness (1825–1894), New York City, 1850's. Inness portrays Sunnyside in a tangle of trees and vines in the typical romantic Hudson River Valley style.

28. *Summer Afternoon, Sunnyside,* watercolor, by John Henry Hill (1839–1922), New York, 1878. Although painted considerably after Irving's death, this drawing gives a detailed picture of Sunnyside and its architecture.

Sunnyside was one of the most popular houses for pictorial representation in its day. Both Washington Irving and Sunnyside were painted and photographed by many of the leading American artists who were friends of Irving or who journeyed to Sunnyside because of its literary importance. The house was also the subject of lithographs by Currier and Ives that were distributed in great numbers throughout the country. The entire property at Sunnyside was landscaped in the Romantic manner; it had a large pond which Irving called his "Little Mediterranean." From it ran a stream which joined another branch to create a waterfall that dropped through a highly picturesque chasm and eventually flowed into an inlet of the Hudson in front of the house.

29. *Sunnyside,* colored lithograph published in
New York in the late nineteenth century.
Sunnyside became a national literary shrine through
mass circulation of this lithograph, published by
Currier & Ives in two sizes.

After Irving died at Sunnyside on November 28,
1859, the property passed to his nieces, Catherine and
Sarah, who for years had acted as his hostesses. The
house remained unchanged for many years, but in 1896 a
collateral descendant acquired the property and added a
large Tudor wing to the north side of the house. At the
same time several small rooms were removed from the
house while the buildings in the kitchen yard at the rear
were razed.

The property stayed in the Irving family until 1945
when it was acquired for John D. Rockefeller, Jr. The
house was opened to the public in 1947 with the wing

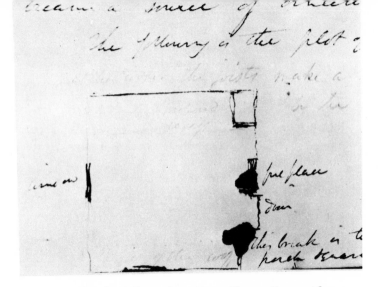

32. *Sketch of floor plan, Guest Room, Sunnyside,* by Washington Irving.

steps' and projecting eaves, so that I presume there will not be any glaring incongruity in it. I wish to know how the windows are to be glazed, that is to say, what is to be the minute directions. Give me your ideas, both for the dormer windows at the west end and the other windows which have but two casements.

I am thinking of having the bedroom in the west and upstairs finished in a different way from the others, that is to say, not arched, but a recess made at the end adjoining the small center bedroom; and the other end of the room left with the natural pitch of the roof. The recess at the end would be so made as to hide the slope of the roof at the angle made by the front and rear building and to gain to the room the full height up to the beams— At the opposite end where there is the pitch of the roof, a light arch might be made along the ceiling, just at the break of the roof, and beneath at the slope of the roof might be papered with striped paper, so as to resemble the curtain of a tent—I do not know whether I make myself understood. I have seen an irregular attic room managed in that way in France, with a very pretty effect. The very irregularity became a source of ornament.

The following is a plot of the room as you laid it out. By the plan here suggested the room will gain the full height of the rafters throughout, except at the slope of the front porch—I think I have given you explanation enough to perplex and confound you, so let me hear from you forthwith and believe me very truly yours

Washington Irving[6]

As a housewarming present for Irving, his friend, Gouverneur Kemble, decided to present him with two iron benches to go on either side of the entrance door at Sunnyside. These were to be cast at Kemble's West Point iron foundry in Cold Spring-on-Hudson. In a letter dated November 14, 1836, Irving again wrote to George Harvey:

Mr. Gouverneur Kemble, who was at my cottage a few days since, offered to furnish me with two gothic (sic) seats of cast iron for the porch, and to have them cast in the highlands, if I would send him patterns. You were kind enough to say you would give me designs for the seats; I will be much obliged to you if you will do so at your leisure & convenience. I should like the backs to incline a little and to be smooth at the top so as to admit of a lounging position, and to be leaned upon.[7]

Included in this letter are two drawings from the hand of Washington Irving, one of which is very similar to the existing benches with Gothic tracery and arches as details. (Plates 33, 34)

The entrance hall has a cool, rather sombre atmosphere; the floor is made of Minton tiles which exactly match a kind very much advocated by the American tastemaker, Andrew Jackson Downing (1815–1852).

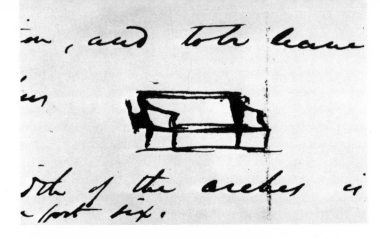

33. *Sketch of cast iron bench for Sunnyside,*
by Washington Irving, in letter to George Harvey
dated November 14, 1836. Collection of New York
Public Library. Bench was proposed, never executed.

34. *Sketch of cast iron bench for Sunnyside,*
by Washington Irving, in letter to George Harvey
dated November 15, 1836. In collection of New
York Public Library. This bench was cast by
Gouverneur Kemble at the West Point foundry,
Cold Spring-on-Hudson. He gave Irving a pair of
them as a housewarming present.

The study at Sunnyside was certainly the heart of the house, for it was here that Irving spent long hours at work and received most of his callers. The design of the room was highly romantic in its concept: at one end was a draped alcove which contained a divan with loose pillows against a wall of books. Irving actually used this room as a kind of one-room apartment during the first ten years of his occupancy of Sunnyside. It was only in 1847, when additions were made to the house, that Irving moved to an upstairs bedroom. The partner's desk at which he sat was given to him by G. P. Putnam, his publisher. A silver label attached to the desk is engraved "Washington Irving from his publishers, Feb. 27, 1856."

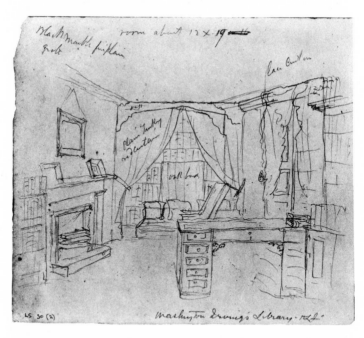

35. *Drawing of Washington Irving's Study, Sunnyside,* thought to be by Benson J. Lossing (1813–1891), in Lossing Collection of the Henry E. Huntington Library and Art Gallery, San Marino, California.

An interesting drawing considered to be by the hand of the writer Benson J. Lossing shows the room in considerable detail. (Plate 35) On either side of the mantelpiece hangs a pair of framed wash drawings by George Cruikshank (1791–1878) which are illustrations for *A History of New York . . . by Diedrich Knickerbocker*. On March 16, 1860, Irving's painter friend, Daniel Huntington (1816–1906), did a series of three pencil sketches of the study; they were a view of the desk at the south end of the room, the fireplace wall, and a single drawing of the curious desk chair in the late classical style which Irving always used. (Plates 36, 37, 38) The books in the study all belonged to Irving, and the author was portrayed by many painters seated at the desk there.

36. *Washington Irving's Library,* pencil drawing by
Daniel Huntington (1816–1906). Dated March 16,
1860. Courtesy: The Cooper-Hewitt Museum of
Decorative Arts and Design, Smithsonian Institution.

37. *Library, Sunnyside,* drawing by Daniel Huntington. Dated March 16, 1860. The Cooper-Hewitt Museum of Decorative Arts and Design, Smithsonian Institution.

38. *Washington Irving's Study Chair,* pencil drawing by Daniel Huntington. March 15, 1860. Courtesy: The Cooper-Hewitt Museum.

Benson Lossing's *The Hudson, from the Wilderness to the Sea* was published in 1866. (Plates 39, 40) The work included an engraving of the study with the following description:

I visited Sunnyside again only a fortnight before the death of Mr. Irving. I found him in his study, a small, quiet room, lighted by two delicately curtained windows, one of which is seen nearest the porch, in our little sketch of the (exterior) of the mansion, from the window he could see far down the river; from the other, overhung with ivy, he looked out upon the lawn and the carriage-way from the lane. In a curtained recess was a lounge with cushions, and books on every side. A large easy-chair, and two or three others, a writing-table with many drawers, shelves filled with books, three small pictures, and 2 neat bronze candelabra, completed the furniture of the room. It was warmed by an open grate of coals in a black variegated marble chimney-piece. Over this were three small pictures. The larger represents "A literary party at Sir Joshua Reynolds." The other two were spirited little pen & ink sketches, with a little colour-illustrative of scenes in one of the earlier of Mr. Irving's works—"Knickerbocker's History of New York"—which he picked up in London many years ago. One represented Stuyvesant confronting Rising, the Swedish governor; the other, Stuyvesant's wrath in council.[8]

39. *Irving's Study,* from Benson Lossing's *The Hudson from the Wilderness to the Sea,* Troy, New York, 1866.

40. Washington Irving's Study, Sunnyside. It
remains today, exactly as it was
during his lifetime. Comparison of this
twentieth-century picture with documentation
provided in illustrations 35 through 39 will show
that most of the original material is in place.

The dining room on the west side of the house contains mahogany Sheraton dining chairs with Gothic Revival backs which belonged to Irving. (Plate 41) On the wall hangs William J. Hubard's (1807–1862) portraits of Mr. and Mrs. John Pendleton Kennedy, who were frequent visitors at Sunnyside. (Plates 42, 43) Kennedy, a Marylander, was known as a diplomat, politician, and writer.

41. Dining Room, Sunnyside, showing the dining chairs with Gothic backs and the Voltaire chair near the window. The silk damask drapes at the window and the lace curtains under them are nineteenth-century. In combination with the green carpet they provide a particularly elegant setting for the room.

An interesting quotation documents the existence of these portraits in the dining room. One of Irving's guests wrote an article in *The Home Journal* in 1859 which said:

> We had two 'Mr. Kennedys' in the dining room . . . our friend's portrait, as he sat at the dining-table, hanging directly over his head.

42. *John Pendleton Kennedy* (1795–1870), oil on wood panel, attributed to William James Hubard (c. 1807–1862), Richmond, Virginia, c. 1831.

43. *Elizabeth Gray Kennedy* (Mrs. John P. Kennedy), oil on canvas, attributed to William James Hubard (c. 1807–1862), Richmond, Virginia, c. 1831–1832.

Irving purchased much of the glass, ceramics and silver for the dining room during his long periods of residence in Europe. (Plate 44) Irving wrote his niece, Miss Sarah Irving, from Madrid on September 28, 1842:

> I recently received my books and papers that were forwarded from America and I think these the articles of silver that were put up by you at the cottage. I now only want some plated ware and cutlery which are on their way from England, to set me out completely. All my china, glass, linen, etc. purchased at Paris came here in perfect order. They were all purchased by Mr. Storrow and are a credit to his judgement and good taste. They are simple but eloquent.[9]

44. Candlesticks, pair, possessions of Washington Irving, Sheffield plate, in neo-classical style, England, early nineteenth century.

The parlor was a center of family life. It was here that Irving's nieces, Catherine and Sarah, played the square rosewood piano made by Robert Nunns, Clark and Company of New York City. (Plate 45) Hanging above the piano is a steel engraving of Sir Walter Scott and his literary circle at Abbotsford, a gift from the Scottish bard to Irving. (Plate 46) Another beautiful view of the river is to be seen from the windows of this room. (Plate 47) The portrait of the young Irving by John Wesley Jarvis (1780–1840) seems to preside over the entire room, while a smaller pencil drawing of Irving at middle age, which bears the monogram of the English painter Sir Thomas Lawrence, offers excellent evidence of Irving's intimate

45. Piano, of rosewood, by Robert Nunns, Clark & Co., New York City, c. 1833–1838. Irving purchased this piano for his nieces, and it was often the center of musical activity in the parlor.

friendship with artistic circles in England. All of the pictures hanging in the small picture gallery at the far end of the parlor belonged to Irving. Many of these are original drawings done by famous artists of the day to serve as illustrations for *The Alhambra, Knickerbocker's History of New York,* and other works.

46. *Sir Walter Scott and his Literary Friends at Abbotsford,* mezzotint engraving on paper by James Faed after the painting by Thomas Faed, (1826–1900), Edinburgh, Scotland, 1854. This mezzotint was given to Irving by Sir Walter Scott.

47. View of Parlor, Sunnyside. The ochre walls and
light brown trim give this room a bright feeling
as was intended by nineteenth-century tastemakers.
Much of the furniture here is original.

The food for the dining table was prepared on an iron cooking range in the kitchen at the rear of the house. (Plate 48) The range was a convenience installed late in Irving's life as was the iron sink with water running by gravitational flow. The kitchen and pantries contain all of the paraphernalia needed for cooking the large dinners so popular at the time.

48. View of Kitchen, Sunnyside. When Irving moved to Sunnyside cooking was still done on the open hearth. It was not until later in his life that the cast iron cooking range was installed. The kitchen contains such advanced items as a copper boiler for heating water and a cast iron sink with hot and cold running water.

Upstairs is a unique arrangement of the interior architecture of the rooms. Irving devised sloping barrel ceilings and ingenious arches which were incorporated into a pleasing whole. The room where Irving died is in the southeast corner of the upstairs. (Plate 49) It contains a tester Sheraton bed which, tradition says, belonged to Irving and also a number of his personal effects. His walking stick and several pictures are among these.

49. Washington Irving's Bedroom, Sunnyside. Irving moved to this room after the tower was completed in 1847. The bed in the neo-classical style was probably brought from Irving's New York City residence.

The print, "Christus Consolator," was one of Irving's favorite possessions and the two engravings of Saracens were reminders to Irving of his period of life in Spain. (Plates 50, 51) Irving's nephew, Pierre Munro Irving, took care of his uncle during the last months of his life and stayed in the tiny bedroom over the front door. An airy room with light coming in from three sides, it was often used as a storeroom for the books and papers Irving needed for writing.

50. *Christus Consolator,* engraving, published by
Goupil & Vibert from a painting attributed to
Ary Scheffer (1795–1858), Paris, c. 1848. Irving
purchased this from a gallery in New York City
and greatly admired the engraving.

51. *Officier Circassien,* lithograph attributed to Lehnert, France, c. 1850. It is thought that Irving purchased this in Europe and brought it to Sunnyside with him.

52. Guest Room, Sunnyside. Painted cottage furniture is used. Furniture of this type was extremely popular for use in country houses. The arch with striped paper behind can be seen here.

The guest room contains two arched alcoves. (Plates 52, 53) One is papered in a striped pattern, for it is known that Irving wrote about them from New York City to George Harvey in 1835 in a letter previously quoted. Surely this reveals another aspect of the interests of the Romantic nineteenth-century man. The room is furnished in painted cottage furniture favored by A. J. Downing. A set of it is shown in his book *The Architecture of Country Houses* (1850). A description of this type of furniture is given on the following page.

53. North side of Guest Room, Sunnyside. The bed alcove contains a small door which allows daylight to come in from a skylight in the hall.

This furniture is remarkable for its combination of lightness and strength, and for its essentially cottage-like character. It is very highly finished, and is usually painted drab, white, gray, a delicate lilac, or a fine blue —the surface polished and hard, like enamel. Some of the better sets have groups of flowers or other designs painted upon them with artistic skill. When it is remembered that the whole set for a cottage bedroom may be had for the price of a single wardrobe in mahogany, it will be seen how comparatively cheap it is.[10]

Farther down the upstairs hall are the rooms occupied by Irving's brother, Ebenezer, and his two nieces. Ebenezer's room is furnished in spartan manner, the dark green paint of the furniture strongly contrasting with the ochre paint of the walls. (Plate 54) Here the furniture is the type that would have been made by the local cabinet-maker; many of the accessories used in the room belonged to Ebenezer.

54. View of Ebenezer Irving's Bedroom, Sunnyside. Irving's older brother's taste was quite somber. It is reflected in the relatively simple furnishings of the room.

55. The Tower Bedroom, Sunnyside. This room was occupied
by a member of Irving's family when there were
more guests than the house could accommodate.

The nieces' room strikes a note of gaiety, for there
is a floral patterned carpet with colorful flowers. The
larger mahogany sleigh bed, chest of drawers, and sewing
stands are all typical of the furnishings of the room of a
fashionable lady of that day. A guest room at the rear of
the upstairs contains a remarkable cast-iron bed with
Gothic decorative details which was probably made at
one of the foundries along the Hudson. The area in the
tower, or "Pagoda," because of the nature of its use, is
furnished more simply than other rooms in the house.
The rooms on the first floor were used by servants, while
the comfortable room on the second floor was generally
occupied by a member of Irving's family who had relin-
quished a room in the other part of the house. (Plate 55)
The top floor under the eaves was used for storage.

In order to run a country retreat it was necessary to have stables, barns, a greenhouse, and other service buildings on the property. The kitchen yard at the rear of the house has been carefully restored to its appearance during Irving's time through the use of documentary sources. (Plate 56) A root cellar with two levels stored vegetables, meat, and milk; the wood shed held kitchen and fireplace fuel.

56. Tower and kitchen yard at Sunnyside. This view of the rear of Sunnyside gives another romantic view of the angles and corners which make the house unique.

An ice house was used for summer storage of ice cut from the pond in winter. (Plate 57) This building was drawn by Evie Todd, c. 1850, a local schoolgirl, in an album of area scenes. The view from the top of the tower is difficult to see because of the placement of the windows.

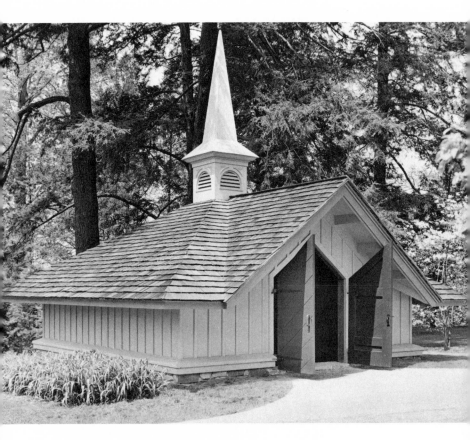

57. Ice House, Sunnyside. The spire on the ice house is derivative of Gothic revival design and provides a focal point in the kitchen yard.

Gnarled wisteria vines, dating from Irving's time, cover
the entrance to Sunnyside. Three weather vanes, which
Irving collected, still sway in the breezes above his home.

As early as the tenth century vanes in the shape of
roosters were used on churches to recall
St. Peter's betrayal of Christ: "The cock shall not crow
this day, before that thou shalt thrice deny that thou
knowest me." Early American folk artists were perhaps more
concerned with the barnyard rooster's alerting call.

Banners and pennants were also commonly used as vanes,
dating from medieval practice. The pennant, bearing the
date 1765 and balanced by a wild dove, is a replica of the
original, a gift to Irving from Gill Davis, whom he referred
to as the "King of Coney Island." Irving wrote that Davis
had retrieved the vane from a demolished windmill in Rotterdam.

The racing horse, swift and free, became a popular
symbol for weather vanes in the mid-nineteenth century,
particularly as the sport of trotting developed here.

Sunnyside's buildings alone do not make it the romantic place it is. The walks that meander through the property afford magnificent views of the forest and the river. A path down the bank at the front of the house takes the visitor to a delightful waterfall fed by Sunnyside brook. Further walks through the woods are bordered by wild flowers of the same variety as those that bloomed there in Irving's time. The marvelous trees, many of them old when Irving purchased the property, stand in the same manner and profusion as when they were painted by mid-nineteenth-century artists.

Irving must have enjoyed his life at Sunnyside, which he called his "snuggery." Sunnyside has always been one of the most beloved places in America and to Europeans, and it is certainly one of the best known American houses. It has been a haven of peace and contentment and the site of gentle, gracious living. (Plate 58) Above all, though, Sunnyside reflects the highly personal taste of Washington Irving. This is sensed in every part of the property.

58. *Washington Irving and His Literary Friends at Sunnyside,*
    oil on canvas, by Christian Schussele (1824 or 1826–1879),
    Philadelphia, 1863. Shown left to right are: Henry T. Tuckerman,
    Oliver Wendell Holmes, William Gilmore Simms,
    Fitz-Greene Halleck, Nathaniel Hawthorne,
    Henry Wadsworth Longfellow, Nathaniel Parker Willis,
    William H. Prescott, Washington Irving, James Kirke Paulding,
    Ralph Waldo Emerson, William Cullen Bryant,
    John Pendleton Kennedy, James Fenimore Cooper, and
    George Bancroft. Painted after Irving's death, this grouping
    of people was imagined by Schussele.

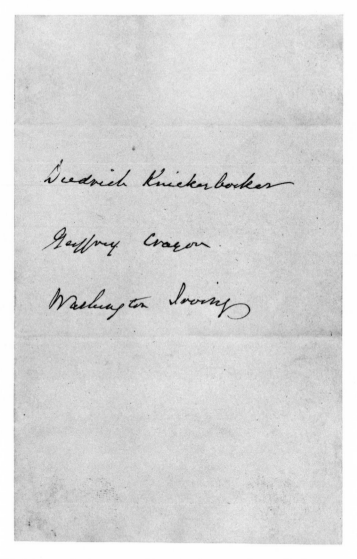

Washington Irving wrote his own signature beneath those
of his two most famous pen names—Diedrich Knickerbocker
and Geoffrey Crayon—on a slip of note paper. The manuscript
is now in the Berg Collection of The New York Public Library.

Like other Romantics of his day, Irving paid special attention
to the landscaping of the grounds around his home.
Andrew Jackson Downing, the founder of American landscape
architecture, admired the rural effect, "that assists in making up
the charm of the whole." The views here are of the
"Little Mediterranean," Irving's picturesque name for the pond
that is near the modern Reception Center.

Path to the Cottage from the River

The Pond

Up River from the Lawn

The pencil drawings reproduced here are part of a series
of twelve, executed by T. Addison Richards (1820-1900)
who made a visit to Sunnyside on September 18-20, 1855.
These are the original drawings he did for a careful descriptive
article which he wrote for *Harper's New Monthly Magazine*
(December 1856) about Sunnyside and Washington Irving's
life there. The article and the drawings provide an intimate
picture of the property just prior to Irving's death.

On November 30, 1859, two days after Irving's death, the Common Council of the City of New York adopted this official memorial document, calling for church and fire alarm bells to be tolled and flags flown at half mast on the day of the funeral.

In The Churchyard At Tarrytown

Here lies the gentle humorist, who died
In the bright Indian Summer of his fame!
A simple stone, with but a date and name,
Marks his secluded resting-place beside
The river that he loved and glorified.
Here in the autumn of his days he came,
But the dry leaves of life were all aflame
With tints that brightened and were multiplied.
How sweet a life was his; how sweet a death!
Living, to wing with mirth the weary hours,
Or with romantic tales the heart to cheer;
Dying, to leave a memory like the breath
Of summers full of sunshine and of showers,
A grief and gladness in the atmosphere.

HENRY WADSWORTH LONGFELLOW
(1876)

Among the outpouring of tributes to Irving after his
death were many from the leading authors of the nineteenth
century. This poem by Henry Wadsworth Longfellow is one
of the most touching of the farewells.

CHRONOLOGY*

1783   April 3, born in New York City.

1802   Enters law office of former Attorney General Josiah Ogden Hoffman.

1802–03   Contributes nine essays by "Jonathan Oldstyle, Gent." to the *Morning Chronicle* newspaper.
Travels to the St. Lawrence River and Montreal.

1804–06   Travels in Europe.

1806   March 24, arrives at New York;
Nov. 21, passes state bar examination.

1807–08   Contributes pseudonymously to *Salmagundi*, published in 20 numbers.

1809   Dec. 6, "Diedrich Knickerbocker's" *A History of New York* published in the United States.

1812–14   Edits the *Analectic Magazine* published in Philadelphia.

1814   In autumn, serves as colonel of state militia and aide to Gov. Daniel D. Tompkins.

1815   May 15, sails to England. Family import firm in Liverpool bankrupt in 1818; Irving turns to professional authorship.

1819–20   *The Sketch Book of Geoffrey Crayon, Gent.* published serially in the United States; 1820, two volumes published in England.

1822   *Bracebridge Hall* published. Irving resides in Dresden.

1824   *Tales of a Traveller* published.

1826   Moves from Paris and Bordeaux to Madrid at invitation of the American Minister.

1828–29   Resides in Seville and Granada.

*From Myers, Andrew B. (Ed.). The Worlds of Washington Irving. (Sleepy Hollow Restorations, Tarrytown [N. Y.], 1974).

1828   *Life and Voyages of Christopher Columbus* published.

1829   *The Conquest of Granada* published. Appointed
Secretary to the U. S. Legation in London.

1831   Receives an honorary Doctor in Civil Law (D.C.L.)
degree conferred by Oxford University. *Voyages and
Discoveries of the Companions of Columbus* published.

1832   *The Alhambra* published. May, returns to New York.
Tours western part of country.

1835   *The Crayon Miscellany* published in three parts.

1836   *Astoria* published. Settles into Sunnyside,
purchased the year before.

1837   *The Adventures of Captain Bonneville* published.

1838   Declines President Van Buren's offer of cabinet post,
and also Tammany Hall nomination as Mayor of New York.

1841   *Biography . . . of Margaret Davidson* published.

1842   Appointed Minister to Spain and reaches
Madrid, July 25.

1846   Returns to Sunnyside.

1848   Publication begins by G. P. Putnam of the Author's
Revised Edition of Irving's works, to be completed in 15
volumes in 1851. It includes a revised *Oliver Goldsmith* (1849)
and a new *Mahomet and His Successors* (1850).

1849   Feb. 14, elected President of the first Board of Trustees
of the Astor Library. *A Book of The Hudson* published.

1855   *Wolfert's Roost* published, also Volume I of the
Life of George Washington, to be completed by Volumes II
and III (1856), Volume IV (1857), and Volume V (1859).

1859   Nov. 28, dies at Sunnyside. Burial in
Sleepy Hollow Cemetery in Tarrytown.

SELECTED BIBLIOGRAPHY

Aderman, Ralph M. (Ed.). *Washington Irving Reconsidered—A Symposium* (Hartford [Conn.], 1969).

Brooks, Van Wyck. *The World of Washington Irving* (New York, 1944).

Cater, Harold Dean. *Washington Irving and Sunnyside* (Tarrytown [N. Y.], 1957).

Hellman, G. S. *Washington Irving, Esq.* (London, 1924.)

Irving, Pierre M. *The Life and Letters of Washington Irving* 3 vols. (New York, 1869).

Leary, Lewis. *Washington Irving* (Minneapolis [Minn.], 1963).

Myers, Andrew B. *Washington Irving—A Tribute* (Tarrytown, [N. Y.], 1972).

———. (Ed.). *The Knickerbocker Tradition: Washington Irving's New York.* (Tarrytown [N. Y.], 1974).

———. *The Worlds of Washington Irving: From an exhibition of rare book and manuscript materials in the special collections of The New York Public Library.* (Tarrytown [N. Y.], 1974).

Williams, Stanley T. *The Life of Washington Irving* 2 vols. (New York, 1935).

———. "Washington Irving," *Dictionary of American Biography* Vol. 9, pp. 505–511 (New York, 1933).

NOTES

1. Pierre M. Irving, *The Life and Letters of Washington Irving,* (New York, 1869), Vol. I, p. 227.

2. Pierre M. Irving, *The Life and Letters of Washington Irving,* Vol. III, pp. 36-38.

3. G. P. Putnam, "Washington Irving," *Harpers Weekly Supplement,* May 27, 1871, p. 496.

4. Pierre M. Irving, *The Life and Letters of Washington Irving,* Vol. III, pp. 153-154, November 25, 1840; to Mrs. Van Wart.

5. Pierre M. Irving, *The Life and Letters of Washington Irving,* Vol. III, p. 92.

6. Collection, Sleepy Hollow Restorations.

7. Seligman Collection, Volume of autographed letters . . . 1805–1859, The New York Public Library.

8. Benson Lossing, *The Hudson, from the Wilderness to the Sea,* (Troy, N. Y., 1866), p. 344.

9. Letter owned by Dr. Robert Grinnell.

10. A. J. Downing, *The Architecture of Country Houses,* (New York, 1850), p. 415.

BOABDIL
THE LAST KING OF GRANADA

WASHINGTON
IRVING
1783-1859
ESSAYIST POET
HISTORIAN TRAVELER
DIPLOMATIST SOLDIER
THE FIRST AUTHOR OF
OUR REPUBLIC

RIP VAN WINKLE
THE DREAMER OF THE KAATSKILLS

At the entrance to Sunnyside Lane off Route 9, stands the
Washington Irving Memorial, the work of the sculptor
Daniel Chester French. The memorial contains a bronze bust of
Irving flanked by full-length bronze reliefs of two of the most
famous characters in his literary works. The memorial was dedicated
in 1928, and was the gift of Mrs. Henry Black of Irvington.
French, an outstanding artist, also created the Minute Man
Monument in Concord, Mass., and the statue of Abraham Lincoln
in the Lincoln Memorial in Washington, D. C.